Keeping
Clean

WAYLAND

Published in paperback in 2014 by Wayland
Copyright © Wayland 2014

Wayland
338 Euston Road
London NW1 3BH

Wayland Australia
Level 17/207 Kent Street
Sydney NSW 2000

All rights reserved
Senior Editor: Jennifer Schofield
Designer: Sophie Pelham
Digital Colour: Carl Gordon

CIP data:
Gogerly, Liz
  Keeping clean. - (Looking after me)
  1. Hygiene - Juvenile literature
  I. Title
  613.4

 ISBN: 978 0 7502 8266 6

Printed in China

10 9 8 7 6 5 4 3 2 1

Wayland is a division of Hachette Children's Books,
an Hachette UK company.
www.hachette.co.uk

Looking After Me

Keeping Clean

Written by Liz Gogerly
Illustrated by Mike Gordon

WAYLAND

Karim and Kurt loved playing in dirt.
Being mucky was marvellous.
Getting grubby was great.

The dirty pair hated bath time.
Clean clothes felt horrible.

Kurt ran away from hairbrushes.

Karim liked long nails that could scoop up dirt.

They often forgot
to clean their teeth.

But everything changed the day they visited the zoo. It began when they saw the bears.

'Why are they rubbing themselves like that?' asked Kurt. 'To scratch off the dirt,' explained his Dad.

The tigers were licking themselves clean with their bristly tongues.

The monkeys were grooming each other. They picked out the fleas, bits of dirt and left over food.

Even the elephants were washing themselves, spraying water everywhere.

The giraffes' house was really smelly.
But, the zookeeper went in with
his hose and brush.
Soon the giraffes
were much happier.

The zookeeper told the boys about wild animals... Crocodiles have their teeth cleaned by a little bird. It eats the scraps from between the crocodile's sharp teeth.

The boys enjoyed their trip to the zoo.

It made them think about
keeping clean.

If animals could wash themselves
so could they.

Kurt and Karim cleaned up their acts. Now they wash, soap, and dry after they've been to the toilet.

Before and after eating
they clean their hands.

If there isn't any water, they use a special gel instead.

They rub
and rub
until all the
gel is gone.

It's important to get
rid of the germs.

Germs are like little bugs
that live on your skin.

They can make
you very sick.

These days
Kurt takes
more showers.

Karim's discovered that baths
can be lots of fun.

Afterwards, it's important to dry from head to toe. If they don't, their skin might itch.

Then they put on lovely, clean pyjamas. They feel soft and smell fresh.

These days Kurt brushes his teeth every morning and night.

Karim lets his dad cut his nails. Short nails are cleaner and have less germs.

Each morning they put
on clean underwear
and clothes.

Once a week they both
get out the shampoo.
It makes their hair shine.

Then it's off to have fun and
get covered in mud and muck,
grass stains and scuffs.

NOTES FOR PARENTS AND TEACHERS

SUGGESTIONS FOR READING **LOOKING AFTER ME: KEEPING CLEAN** WITH CHILDREN

Keeping Clean is the story of two boys called Kurt and Karim. Like many young children they try to avoid washing, having their hair and teeth brushed and having their nails trimmed. The story begins with a few amusing scenes where the boys' parents attempt to groom their wayward sons. After reading this early section you could discuss with the children their own personal hygiene habits. This could be quite a lively debate as children love to talk about being dirty and grubby.

Kurt and Karim change their attitude towards keeping clean when they visit the zoo. The children may have their own experiences of watching animals groom themselves. They could talk about how their pets keep clean. Possibly, they've seen birds taking dust baths in the garden. Talking about animals is always a good way of getting children to open up on a subject. This would be a useful way of starting a discussion about why the children think it is important to keep clean.

It is important for children to learn when to wash their hands and how to do this properly. The book has different examples of Kurt and Karim washing their hands. The children may have other examples of when to wash their hands, too. This is a good time to talk to the children about germs and infections and how keeping themselves and especially their hands clean helps to prevent illnesses.

By the end of the book Kurt and Karim enjoy bathing and grooming and know the reasons why they should keep clean. However, it's important that children are allowed to explore the world around them. Getting dirty is part of that process and there is rarely any harm in getting covered in dirt, if they have a good wash afterwards!

LOOKING AFTER ME AND THE NATIONAL CURRICULUM

The Looking After Me series of books is aimed at children studying PSHE at Key Stage 1. In the section *Knowledge, Skills and Understanding: Developing a Healthy, Safer Lifestyle* of the National Curriculum, it is stated that pupils are expected to 'learn about themselves as developing individuals and as members of their communities, building on their own experiences and on the early learning goals for personal, social and emotional development'.

Children are expected to learn:
- how to make simple choices that improve their health and well-being to maintain personal hygiene;
- how some diseases spread and can be controlled;
- about the process of growing from young to old and how people's needs change;
- the names of the main parts of the body;
- that all household products, including medicines, can be harmful if not used properly;
- rules for, and ways of, keeping safe, including basic road safety, and about people who can help them to stay safe.

BOOKS TO READ

Health Choices: Keeping Clean Cath Senker (Wayland, 2004)

Me and My Body: Why Wash? Claire Llewellyn (Wayland, 2008)

Dirty Bertie David Roberts (Little Tiger Press, 2003)

ACTIVITY

Using the examples of the bears, tiger, monkeys and crocodiles in this book, ask children to look for pictures of different animals cleaning themselves. They could find examples of both domestic animals, such as cats that lick themselves, or wild animals, such as buffaloes that have a secretary bird to pick bugs from their hides.

INDEX